TERRIBLE TRAUMA
LIKE A POEM

Rosemarie M. Neilson LCSW AC

authorHOUSE®

AuthorHouse™
1663 Liberty Drive
Bloomington, IN 47403
www.authorhouse.com
Phone: 1 (800) 839-8640

Published by AuthorHouse 10/10/2019

ISBN: 978-1-7283-3131-7 (sc)
ISBN: 978-1-7283-3129-4 (hc)
ISBN: 978-1-7283-3130-0 (e)

Library of Congress Control Number: 2019916173

I thought about telling you about how you have impressed me, how you motivated me, how you have helped me see the difference you've made in my life in 27 years so long yet it seems it is not. There's so many memories but they're all filled with hope. That's what I want you all to remember. I want you to remember hope.

I will love you always.

POEMS OF THE GREAT WAR

IN FLANDERS FIELDS

In Flanders fields

by John McCrae, May 1915

In Flanders fields the poppies blow
Between the crosses, row on row,
That mark our place; and in the sky
The larks, still bravely singing, fly
Scarce heard amid the guns below.

We are the Dead. Short days ago
We lived, felt dawn, saw sunset glow,
Loved and were loved, and now we lie

We're here today to talk about stress, when we think of stress we think of stressors.....just identifying stressors doesn't get rid of stress. What we need to do is find the origin of the stressors. Easier said than done.

For most of our lives we seem to go from one level of development to the next totally oblivious to how we got there...unless of course stressors get in our way.

Stress is a reaction, an action and a behavior....

All organisms respond to stress. The life cycle of all organisms depends on stress. Stress is cause and effect. Stress is change.

And those organisms that best respond to stress....survive! Adaptation ....but unlike lower organisms the human person is composed of body, mind, and spirit.

And it is this unique composition that makes our life form so magnificent.....and so enormously complex.

If we were only physical form...we would not have the problems we encounter with stress...it is our humanness that is experienced through our mind or our intellect, and through our soul or spirit that causes us psychological dilemma...this is where we get in trouble.

The intellect, the body and the spirit all develop at different cycles. (Use examples)

Scientists measure stages of physical growth and development. Theorists such as Eric Erikson, Piaget, and Freud, measure psychological growth.

Eric Erikson defined emotional development in 8 segments:

> Birth to age 1 ½ Trust vs. mistrust
> 1 ½ to age 3 Autonomy vs. shame & doubt
> 3 to 5 ½ Initiative vs. guilt
> 5 ½ to 12 (Ego) Industry vs. inferiority
> 13 to 18 Identity vs. role confusion
> 18 to 21 Intimacy vs. isolation
> Early to middle adulthood-Generativity Stagnation
> Late adulthood Ego integrity vs. despair

Now what does all this have to do with stress?

If everyone here in this room is between the ages of 30 to 60 .....we are at the stage of generativity vs. stagnation. Now there a trick to this....

if we did not complete the stage before this one, we have to go back and do it....does anyone tell us this? These stages of development are dependent on the previous stage and how we completed it. So the most crucial stage of course is the first.....trust vs. mistrust.....when we are just born to age 1 ½....

Who is taking care of us at that time? That's when we need everything....if no one took care of us we would just shrivel up and die..... some infants come close to that with what is called failure to thrive. (Use examples)

Most of you are experiencing a good amount of inner turmoil...if you decide to follow your emotions and values many of you will find you are in conflict with your family and their values...is this sounding familiar... can you remember your turbulence in adolescence and conflicts with your values and that of your parents..identity vs. role confusion.....you're not exactly back at square one, but you are back to rethink that role. You can make a different decision now, in fact you will make a different decision now....hopefully without the guilt.

Again depending on how you completed the trust vs. mistrust stage...will you be able to trust your own decisions.....if you did not get permission to trust then autonomy will be very difficult.

Now suppose as a child you got past the stage of shame and doubt, but stumbled on initiative...because you were never allowed to try and fail..and try again. The fear of failure or of making the wrong decision will weigh heavily on you. If that happens then go back and try a bunch of things, things you always wished you could do. Remember that what you do, what you think, and what you feel have to match. (Use examples)

One way to check yourself to see if your ego is integrated is to check what Ego state you are in. During the 1940's psychiatrists, and theorists tried to find out what made psychoanalysis work...so what they identified were three ego states...the Parent....the Adult...and the Child..and they designed a means of measuring this and Eric Berne called it:

Transactional Analysis. So at any given time we think and talk and feel anyone of these three ego states. (Use examples)

In addition to these ego states we also use passive, assertive or aggressive styles of communication. So where do we learn this stuff...we learn most of it before we ever go to school....all in our primary group

The Menninger Clinic in Topeka, Kansas looked at early trauma.. they found that trauma alters brain chemistry, bio feedback. Early trauma causes us to be developmentally fixated, the earlier the trauma, the poorer the prognosis, there is a predisposition to develop a personality disorder. An example would be childhood sexual abuse. This is not motivated by sex but rather a need to control, to have power over someone who has no power, it is to humiliate, to shame. After the trauma shame develops... children always blame themselves...it is never the child's fault.

If you would look at you notes, there a two stress cycles; DISTRESS AND WELLNESS So where does stress come from? (Read)

Some biological factors not included predispose us to disease. Such as anxiety disorders...(Use examples) these are inherited in our DNA. Also predisposing us to lack of wellness is diabetes, heart disease, again inherited. In the limbric system of the cerebral cortex of the brain is the seat of emotions...here neurotransmitters/chemical messengers produce Dopomine, and Seratonin. When these chemicals are lacking, our sense of well being is lacking, we feel down, have low energy, prolonged periods in this condition, lead many of us to depression. And we can do the same thing artificially through drugs and alcohol. You have heard of uppers and downers, well too much alcohol is a downer...it drops our mood, drops our inhibition. Women in menopause have an especially hard time with alcohol...since we are not producing adequate estrogen..we already have a variable mood, due to hormone imbalance and alcohol lowers our threshold to stress. During menopause for many women there is very poor sleep, there are many sleep remedies that work there is no need to suffer from chronic fatigue. Prolonged periods of sleep deprivation can lead to depression. There are numerous vitamins, and herbals to investigate for natural balance. The immune system becomes compensated during menopause, estrogen helps to keep the immune system functioning, again check out therapies that support the immune system to maximize health.

When we do not feel well physically, dealing with stress is often overwhelming. And if we are still carrying around emotional baggage from our childhoods, we need to figure out where we are stuck. Stress is not so much about the situation but rather how we think about the

situation. For many of us our childhoods leave us emotionally crippled... but we don't have to stay that way.

What is some of the emotional baggage...Adult children of alcoholics... do you know that 50% ....50% of all people were raised in an alcoholic household. (Use examples) Living in an alcoholic household is like living in a mine field...you never know when the next bomb is going to explode. It creates dependent and codependent personalities, it creates a high fear of abandonment, a profound betrayal of trust...there we go again,....at trust vs mistrust. Age 0 to 1 ½. We always guess at what is right, over react or under react. Haven't we paid enough.

Activity: Close your eyes...walk down a corridor.....

Questions...what did you see

It's time to do some grieving for yourselves...for the little girls we were.......think of a memory of your childhood... of absolute joy....what was it? (Wait)

We handle stress when we change our perception of ourselves...and I have just the activity to do that......

JUNKANOO
MEDITATION: Come into this my dwelling place
IMAGERY: WALK ON THE BEACH

ON EAGLE'S WINGS

BY MICHAEL JONCAS

1. You who dwell in the shelter of the Lord, who abide in his shadow for life, say to the Lord: "My refuge, my rock in whom I trust!"

REFRAIN: And he will raise you up on eagle's wings, bear you on the breath of dawn, make you to shine like the sun, and hold you in the palm of his hand.

March 22, 2002

Rosemarie Neilson
30 Yerrington Ave.
Norwich, CT 06360

Your March 13, 2002 Position Statement governing the Statute of limitations on child sexual abuse was heroic and long overdue. I commend the Editors for urging laws and legislation to protect the rights of children for safety, and removing barriers which limit criminal prosecution.

As a society our future is our children. Our survival is dependent on our children's future decision making, on their integrity, and on their ability to form right judgement. Why would a country with such prosperity have the horrific numbers of child sexual abuse as we do in the United States? Most often it is presumed that abusers are somewhat depraved and non human. The largest numbers of child abusers at least 70%: are someone the child knows, often a care taker, family member. Abusers are portrayed as sexual predators, and pedophiles.

By creating this abnormal image; we in fact protect the abuser. Children are often taught to avoid the predator, or the dangerous person, but never a "trusted friend or family member". Abusers continue to abuse children because the child's caretaker fails to believe the child's cries for help, fears the disruption of the family, and fears society's disapproval. There are three critical factors that determine the gravity of damage that sexual abuse has on the child: the younger the age of the child, the longer the period of abuse, and the degree of relationship the abuser has with the child. More profound devastation is the threat of physical harm to the child's caretaker, the loss of the relationship, the fear of retaliation, exposure, blame, the loss of trust and exposure to other abusers. For many children there are multiple abusers.

The sexual, emotional and physical abuse of children has been described by many authors as: soul murder. Physicians have learned that trauma affects the neurodevelopment of the growing child's brain. Since the Hippocampus does not become fully functional until the 4th to 5th. yr of life, and the Prefrontal cortex becomes functional at the 10th.; they have discovered that Trauma exacerbates the ordinary state of alarm-proneness

(Yale studies) creating the potential for Post Traumatic Stress Disorder. The effects of child sexual abuse are life long. The adult survivor is often plagued by significant periods of depression, vigilance, psychic numbing, difficultly forming relationships, chronically low self worth, low self esteem, self abuse, suicide, addictions, etc.

The adult survivor is "tortured" their pain is beyond comprehension. So often their existence is relegated to the shadows of living. We as individuals and a society stand and are irate at terrorism at the taking of our family's lives. We mourn for nameless faces, for unspent potential. Child sexual abuse is no different than terrorism........only.... there is little grief shed for the victim.....and never a memorial to the death of the broken child.

Your calling child sexual abuse a "life-altering crime" is without a doubt accurate and still an under statement. It is ironic that we as a society had laws to protect animals before we had laws to protect children. Our laws remain inadequate. Only the outrage of every single person can begin to heal our damaged children.

With great sorrow,
Rosemarie Neilson

December 22, 2001

Rosemarie Neilson, LCSW AC
30 Yerrington Ave.
Norwich, CT 06360

Carra Leah Hood, Editor Aftermath
Connecticut Trauma Coalition
c/o Connecticut Women's Consortium
205 Whitney Ave.
New Haven, CT 06511

Dear Carra,

I am thrilled to be included in the Anthology on Trauma Survival in Writing! It came as such great news. Thank you so much for the selection.

A brief biography:

I am first of all 'old' pushing 60 and it's pushing back. Have worked in the field of mental health for 15 years as a psychiatric social worker and addictions counselor. I have a Masters degree from U CONN, the School of Social Work. I have been employed at the Wm. W. Backus Hospital since 1989, interned there for one year in 1988, and interned for the Department of Corrections in 1987. At Backus I have a caseload of 200 patients. Many of whom are victims of trauma. Trauma in the form of childhood physical, sexual and emotional, adult all of the same, men and women, individual and groups. Have had some extremely moving experiences in working with this population.

Also I have a private practice, work with the school systems as a consultant, and with area day cares instructing on sexual abuse. Have lectured to groups on a variety of topics. Also have been a presenter on domestic violence, for an NASW conference. Have presented several conferences to the staffs of schools. Have prepared a thoroughly comprehensive piece on this topic (100 pages), slides as well.

My work with trauma, was somewhat accidental, and totally intentional. In most of our rounds (team meetings) at the beginning of

my work, most of the medical staff considered sexual abuse a bi product of the psychiatric illness. And considered the psychiatric illness as the psychosis/neurosis as indigenous to the individual's weakness. As often as someone would disclose a history of trauma it was 'used' as an extension of their neurosis/psychosis. It had very low credibility. Most women were found to be psychotic when in fact they were having flashbacks not hallucinations. This developed into further research on my part, more intent listening, and the development of several groups specifically for trauma survivors. It has been entirely rewarding, emancipating, and excruciatingly sad and painful attending to such horrific violence. My goal is empowerment, no one is free or can live free if anyone still remains 'chained' to years of guilt and shame".

I am also a wife of 38 years, 2 adult daughters 37 and 35. Grand daughters ages 17 and 12 from my daughters first marriage and 2 'new' grand children from her recent second marriage, a boy 8 and a girl 6, adorable. My greatest role is that of a grand mother. I love it the best of all my roles in life.

I began art school in my first year of college, I wanted to design, my parents died, and my career ended. I always sought fulfillment in music and art. Performed in community theater for nearly 10 years, 25 years as a classical music performer. Have made numerous huge banners (over 10 feet) at no charge for many years for ecclesiastical use. Designed clothing for many years, and taught home economics prior to social work. Designed programs, brochures etc.

My poetry writing developed as a result of trauma, and it became a ready tool to move my patients from pain into freedom. Many of the groups would need a shove to consolidate their pain to re- direct it, and as a result I began to write poetry within the group describing their movement.

My oldest daughter is an accomplished artist with a recent show at the Orlando Museum of Art, in Orlando Florida.

I said this was brief but obviously I lied. I am filled with joy for such an honor. Many many thanks. And holiday blessings.

Rosemarie Neilson

My contribution to this publication was the result of trauma work I have done for the past 14 years with survivors of domestic violence, assault and childhood trauma. I have very definite beliefs through research and clinical work of the horrendous effects of trauma on the individual. As a mental health professional, I believe I owe the community a pro -active position on these crimes against children.

As a society, our future is our children. Our survival in the world is dependent on our children's future decision making, on their integrity, and on their ability to form right judgement. Why would a country with such prosperity have the horrific numbers of child sexual abuse victims as we do in the United States?

Most often it is presumed that child abusers are somewhat depraved and non human. The largest number of child abusers; at least 70% is someone the child knows, often a caretaker, trusted friend or family member. Abusers are portrayed as sexual predators, and pedophiles. By creating this abnormal image; we in fact protect the abuser. Children are often taught to avoid the predator, or the dangerous person, but they are never cautioned about "a trusted friend or family member". Abusers continue to abuse children because the child's caretaker fails to believe the child cries for help, may fear the disruption of the family, and fears society's disapproval if labeled.

There are three critical factors that determine the gravity of the damage that sexual abuse has on the child: the younger the age of the child, the longer the period of the abuse, and the degree (a blood tie) of the relationship the abuser has with the child. More profound devastation is the threat of physical harm to the child's caretaker, the loss of the relationship, the fear of retaliation, exposure, blame/shame, the loss of trust, exposure to other abusers, and pressure to recant. For many children there are multiple abusers.

2

The sexual, emotional and physical abuse of children has been described by many authors as "soul murder". Science has learned that trauma affects the neurodevelopment of the growing child's brain. Since the Hippocampus does not become fully functional until the 4th

to the 5th yr. of life, and the Prefrontal cortex becomes functional at the 10th yr; scientists have discovered that trauma exacerbates the ordinary state of alarm-proneness (Yale Uni. Studies), creating the potential for Post Traumatic Stress Disorder. The effects of child sexual abuse are life long. The adult survivor is often plagued by significant periods of depression. They experience vigilance, psychic numbing, difficulty forming relationships, chronically low self worth, low self esteem, self abuse, addictions and suicide.

The adult survivor is "tortured" their pain is beyond comprehension. So often their existence is relegated to the shadows of living. We as individuals, and as a society stand and are irate at terrorism at the taking of our family's lives. We mourn for nameless faces, for unspent potential. Child sexual and physical abuse is no different than terrorism.... only ...there is little grief shed for the victim..and never a memorial to the death of the broken child.

Our laws remain inadequate, only the outrage of every single person can begin to heal our damaged children.

Rosemarie Neilson LCSW AC
Licensed Clinical Social Worker, Addictions Counselor

WRITING AS THERAPY

Writing can be quite cathartic, in all of its forms. I often use writing to help patients to reach out to a another in a relationship with the plan not to send the original letter. Usually there is a great deal of pain or loss in the broken relationship. Trying to speak to someone from whom we are estranged is rarely easy and most often impossible. So writing out one's pain can be therapeutic. Writing even is successful when a loved one has died, and there were words left unspoken, and the leaving unresolved.

Journaling is another form of therapy that allows the patient to write a daily journal of his/her emotions and how they feel "blocked" in self expression.

When a couple is separated and the relationship is coming apart, writing back and forth between the couple, each taking time to read the letters, and correspond only by writing letters back, often helps to open the emotional closeness that once was in the relationship.

Writing poetry is a highly successful form of therapy. It is concrete, allows the individual to express their deepest pain and sorrow. It helps to formulate a plan to recover the "self". Often there is so much pain to contain in one's emotions, but most people who hold in trauma, or repress or suppress it feel it is a burden. Writing the closest words that describe their trauma keeps it on paper and not caught in their emotions.

Repetitive thoughts or pressured thoughts also respond well when they are kept track of on little sticky notes and tacked to a refrigerator. I have the patient keep a count simply by taking a slip of paper and putting it on the refrigerator, count how many times this same thought came up in one day. They also have to practice as each day passes taking control of the unwanted thought with a variety of techniques. (Etc)

CONTENTS

NO PLACES LEFT TO BLEED

BY ROSEMARIE M. NEILSON LCSW AC

Hunched over the steering wheel waiting at the light; the horns let out
the blast

Caught in the middle of time, memories flying in the windows with the
cornfields passing

By rows of bailed hay; laying in the fields of rice paddies bullets skimming
the stench of

Bloodied bodies; broken young men before their prime; he wonders when
it will end in

Plenty of blood he tells himself: barely moving from the last skirmish;
no feeling left in his in

His legs; seeing the flag waving not for him but for the coffins sent on
borrowed time to:

Places like Nebraska, Kansas and Omaha City: tens of thousands of blood
haired young men young

Soldiers laid to rest in bloodied fields in places like "Alemaien"; "Laos"
and "Omaha Beaches"

Stained red with youth not ready to die: not ready to see the faces of God
in the

Killing fields of bold young men in tribute to the nine "elevens" of the
world laying in close

Formation "bodies" side by side at "Tet" The Karmir Rouge" bled lifeless
souls just weaned

Of mother's milk to use their blood for able bodied soldiers Filling" the
ranks with

Borrowed youth lining the bunkers "in close formation" marking the crosses in fields of

Poppies in view of "Gettesburge", "Lynchburg" and "Sumter" raising the stripes, "the

Heroes with hearts of purple on Mystic Land and "Wounded Knee" burning the "Teepees"

With children inside to keep them from freezing "burn them alive echoed the rankings"

Dashing the hopes of pledges for peace "washing the souls no longer existing, swallowed in

Waters "bloodied with marrow" washed in vessels hewn of hard lumber carried on bent

Backs of burrowed transport down broke mountains, hollowed of healing firs and balsam

Slaughtered lean and unadorned in hallowed halls and legions in fields of Heroes Bourn

Here lie the babies: mourned in our Nation the City of Newtown all broken in boxes with

Thousands of shells marking the breathing cloistered forever in time at their "Dying" here lie

The Innocents, here lie the "timeless" here lie the families broken forever severed of "Children"

Spent casings litter the barren hallways: forcing decisions, pleading for safety seeking in

Amnesty, "seeking tolerance" "seeking patience" "seeking the shadows walking the hallways"

Praying for us in "feigned resistance" "paying for us in our shattered indulgence" praying

For Us "in our unrighteous politics" the 5th commandment or 1st Amendment, whatever it be

Let us honor the "Children" "let us "Honor the Families" shattered "of Children" "Carried in Boxes".

By Rosemarie M. Neilson LCSW AC

THE ONLY DEFECTIVE

She lives in morning sunsets; sea gulled ocean fronts
Amassed emotions tugging, crumpled memories lugging
Foot printed Jamaican beaches; wistful wonderings
Cocoon nurturing pebbled; captured in an inkling

But she has olive skin

She has paid the ransom, more than seventy times seven.
Its' debt continues to be metered out in further executions.
Wrapped in a flag of white, the dreams; which maybe could have been,
Speak of no surrender for the tyrant; tortured to the core of being.

But she has olive skin

Rippled watered edges lap sentiments and sting memories.
Fastened still with uncut cords, the enigma waits empty handed.
In awe and trembling of the god-mountain, angers' author assigns the
Unending blame: a task at which he bears the stamp of righteousness.

But she has olive skin

What's left of broken mind and spirit?
Fallen wax lays heaped and molded round a tiny flame
Smoke long carried to the four creations;
A whisper of the wind is all that stands between.

But she has olive skin

As I'm dying and I'm crying for the new life kept from trying,
Groans the borrowed spirit sighing..........who would know?
Arising life of origin's mistake, inhales the god-spirit from pore to pore
Breathes deep; the falling healing fountain.

 3

But I have olive skin

"Anointed fallen man, take comfort in my grace".
"I imaged you to me, you who are my very tears"
"Know no boundaries of my love, I cannot wash you from me"
"In daystars time, I will remember you"

"For you have olive skin".

1000 CROWS

Perched at attention invading barren tree tops
Waiting for the signal
The swarm swells the late afternoon red blue sky
Filling every crevice

They say a sign harboring things to come
Sadness of coming death not faring well in circles
Every perch taken by hawk like creatures
Screeching in high pitched tones of foreboding

Weathered storm barren trees house the unexpected
Occupants, the sirens of impending doom telling
Of the dying of this friend of nature
In the broken silence of the red blue sky

Bursts of steel rimmed clouds surround their feathered edges
Folded on the mantle of the cold draped sky
Chilled night wanderer mourns in
Witness to the dying of this friend of nature

Anguish filled lamenting as the countertenor sings
No more to see the beauty of the sun
As salutations shrill on the black
Painted back drop: of the steel blue sky

JOYCE & PETE

They tell the story of not being able to count 50 cents between them when
they married

Times never got much easier but knowing that someone had your back
was by far

The most secure piece of knowledge that two young people of different
means

Found their way into a life that called on their common strengths and
sacrifices.

One million miles without an accident an achievement to be proud of
raves Pete as the

Words slide off his worried face catching a nervous smile from Joyce
waiting for the

Dreaded news for weeks unknowing of her future, how could she be
without him?

How foolish to think she would leave her house that she spent 40 plus
years organizing.

Now finding no interest in the stacks of unfinished work that would
occupy her energy

Even when all else interrupted her stream of obsessive thinking warding
off the fears of

Failure laying close in her projection of a life disappearing before her
gaze, she couldn't

Let it happen without so much a scream, she couldn't let him go, "now
you get up out of

There" she tells him as he lays in anxiety unable to go through the MRI
watching for his

Dignity as she always watched his needs as he rode miles on unmarked
roads to feed and

House the family, how long ago those concerns occupied his awareness
    why now he
Questions should he be tossed back in time bracing for the worst of
    putting 50 cents

Together nurturing their faithfulness never waiving in fidelity to one another
More so now their collective energy cannot summon the security they
    seek to ward
Off the devastation of losing their own image to the endlessness of death
    keeping guard
Of their likenesses merged and etched on marble solid in a tranquil
    graveyard.

TIRE TRACKS

Shakily trying to stand, touching the back of her head she wipes blood
   from her hair.
More blood drips down her ice cold legs as she struggles to stand in the
   new snow.
Ponders the blood from her head and remembers her head hitting the
   ground as he
yanked her across the car seat dragging her onto the ground into the
   woods.

Throbbing pain doubles her arms clutching herself, for 12 she's tall and
   feels the
sickening wrench her stomach empties onto the ground near her feet.
   Too petrified to
move blinking in the total darkness except for where the moon light juts
   between trees.
Fear kept creeping over her; how would she make her way home in the
   darkness.

She remembered his huge hands with the insignia ring when he opened
   his door asking
directions; holding her tight to the seat telling her to stop crying since
   no one would hear.
She shivered remembering his tearing her under clothes off, and the pain,
   she couldn't
push it out of her mind like she did uncle Joe, seeing the knife blade like
   it was yesterday.

She remembered trying to get away hiding under the porch in her
   nightgown, after he'd
passed her to everyone, the smell was always in her head, the alcohol was
   in her hair.

She didn't know what the smell was when she was 3, but always
remembered uncle Joe,
who chased her under the kitchen table threatening to jab her with the
knife if she moved.

Then her eyes saw the lines in the snow too cold to think she bent down
to trace them tire
tracks she thought pulling herself up; beginning to run out of the woods
tears streaming
down her face, "oh god" she kept saying "oh god you gotta help me"
remembering how
afraid she was under the porch so many years ago, 'oh god' afraid someone
would hear.

Janie is that you called a voice from the kitchen it's 11 o'clock, 'ya ma'
never saying
another word climbing into bed with a towel between her legs to stop
the bleeding,
falling into a drug like sleep startled awake when her cat jumped up next
to her crying
into it's fur knowing she remembered uncle Joe telling her the horrible
sadness of today.

Mama never knew, she never told her, like she never told her about uncle
Joe he said
he'd kill her. She couldn't do much to fix the rips in her clothes clutching
them when
she rocked on the floor next to the chimney stuffing them into where
the brick was loose.
She'd washed the dirt and blood stains as best she could tears wetting the
mangled fabric.

Never wishing she was dead, but couldn't feel any more, couldn't
remember when she
last cried: now the sound of crying wakes her, uneasily putting her feet
to the cold floor.

Walking the few steps to the makeshift cradle searching its' contents
slumping down.

Legs and arms wrapped around herself; rocking side to side certain she
heard the crying.

He was too small with all the scarring to carry to term; they told her, try
again she heard.

The brick cold cement raced up to her vision, she could see the lines like
tire tracks

Melting into each other she felt the falling onto the trolley tracks as they
watched.

Startled beyond her grasp thinking she had slipped but certain she heard
the crying.

UP COUNTRY

What would it take to show you how the browns and yellows
Wash the basins of the residue stained of fallen leaves and sinews

How can you tell they speak to you in whispers layering the roadway
Perched in expectation of the soaring flight amidst the soon forgotten

Never could you count the stretches where the road passes by
Openings; of hollows in the earth's long and narrow trenches

It speaks resoundingly of life before life giving birth becoming
Living wonders with new expectations field upon field across

The fences turning stone upon stone wandering up country
Forming paths of exploration relaxation restoration as

Turning leaves reach the dew on half frozen weighted branches
Emptying ice droplets in the crevices opened

While speaking in forgotten tongues nourishing the burnished images
Of once remembered marshes of the plains

Up country wind the chariots of gods descended forming circles
Cropped in icy patterns in frozen stone formations

ROCK HARD

He bellowed between the whacking of the wheel and the gravel
Falling off the edges of the casings
How did he think I could get the hang of it on the first day
Stop wasting time he yelled; "rock hard" I told you

"Leave it up to you to spoil the carvings", why should I worry over carvings
Wedged in between the fillers they stand like toy soldiers at attention
The foreman rattles the kettle in the formation of the next string
Just as they come off the wheel falling unattended to the soft clay beneath.

"Rock hard" he bellows "how come you're so stupid what will it take
    before you get the
hang of it" voices trailing in the broken dialect of farmers turned stone masons
For all they know I could be a spy and off his mind fades into the excitement
Of wayward wagons and twirling bangles, a boy of thirteen smitten with
    spring

And girls his age and older making passes at him as he shows his new
    muscled back
Labored in the tones of the southern red sands heaped in ready for clay
    moldings
Into blocks fit for the stately houses on the banks where he spied in
    windows late night
Watching the wonders of first puberty escaping his rushing into manhood

SAVING GRACE

Pouring the heated can of creamed corn over the toast she noticed how her aunt's face

Was bruised and her eyes were puffy I almost didn't want to breath it being too much for

Aunt Grace to endure quickly I swallowed up the toast and in a few seconds it was gone

All we had to eat since last night's supper I was so hungry I said I was full not to hurt

Graces' feelings hurrying me across the room putting on my coat and rushed us to the

Door running out the back we could hear him in the front "Grace you get back here"

Yelling into the dark cold night, "bring her back" he yelled even louder now the head

Lights hit us and he began to run yelling into the pitch dark moonlight with head lights

Weaving in and out of the darkness, I peed myself and I could feel the heat on my cold

legs, as I could see the snow on Grace's black hair looking up to see if she was mad for

What I just did holding my hand so tight nearly lifting me off my feet running through

The woods finally losing the added stream of headlights drunk again she said by this time

I was so cold I couldn't feel my feet or my hands trying not to cry, I'd tell myself "one

day I'll have rows of cans of spaghetti and meatballs and a bookshelf full of books yes sir

That's what I'll do" consoling herself trying to put Uncle Joe's abuse out
of her head at
Six she had many hiding places mostly in the woods or under the porch
all cold never

Feeling safe mostly always afraid of what the others would do to her she
swallowed hard
Just coming up on Uncle Bill's front porch Grace motioned her to stay
behind as she
Went forward telling about Uncle Joe's drinking pulling her inside and
yelling for me to
Come on up the stairs on legs that were nearly frozen solid "are you
hungry" he asked

Not wanting to hurt Aunt Grace I said we had eaten "thank you" "let me
get you some
Warm clothes using water to get my frozen socks off that were stuck to
my shoes covered
In snow when my feet began to burn and sting I couldn't keep from crying
even if it
Made no sound too afraid to give away the fear that forever stayed inside
me every hour

Every minute of every day since the beginning of my time never trying
to hurt Aunt
Grace who promised her sister she'd take care of me sleeping in the woods
more nights
Than in the house hiding as far back in the closet that I could to get away
from his
Pawing hands yanking me over the floor boards filling me with splinters
for the money

He got from other dirty men who smelled like him "filthy drunk" Aunt
Grace called him
As Uncle Bill had us get into the back seat of his car seeing the marks on
Grace from the

Insulin needles without Ma's money "she would die" she would say I
  needed to be quiet
On the way back to the house "now you mind yourselves" Uncle Bill said
  and let us out.

LOVING U ALWAYS

Over and over the letters hit by the keys stretch out the words of
lovingualways

More over time and day and year they reach the heavens telling you softly

Telling you sweetly the loving feelings saved for the meeting of heaven
and earth

On the day of your birth on the day your soul was raised from heaven
and earth

THE SACRIFICIAL CHILD

Wanting to scream out loud she hears the words ringing in her head shouting

As loud as she ever imagined for all those years she ached in silence shammed

And abandoned at the wrath of the mother she worshipped seeking approval never

Dispensed to cover the wounds inflicted by hated on this their child unprotected

"So why'd you wait so long" no longer mattering needing it most for years forsaken

Crouching in silence begging for mercy cast in the scullery maid to the manor honor

Thy father echoes the duty champions all for the child they have murdered offered

In sacrifice to quiet the lustings casting her soul to the mercies of evils His will be

Done is what they are praying, she in the meantime is casted in stone in paying the

Penance for the sins of the father living in hatred for her soul that was murdered

Silenced then slaughtered removed from the mainstream taking the least to avoid

Further beatings giving what's left to her soul that is dying God be my savior

Enters her pleading calling the mercies to her wounds which are bleeding begging

For God to forgive indiscretions sanctify me for the soul I have murdered forgive

Me of Jesus and grant incarnation bringing me home to the refuge I've needed

Angels incarnate and soul of all mercy lift me to heaven in the arms of my Savior

YOU'RE MINE NOW

The words rang out through the background clutter, words she always
wanted to hear
Now more than ever why wasn't it fifty years ago, why is she so old,
why now?

How could she belong to anyone "older than the hills" she thought as
she smoothed
Out the bulges at her waist angry with herself that she let herself go not caring

How she looked since nobody was looking anyway, as she caught his eye
looking
At her trying to hide her over lapping on the chair wishing she had dyed
her hair

So very many years had escaped their meeting, longing to be his no
matter how bad
She looked at him his sweetness encompassing her without reservation
without condition

Coming home after so much heartache tears filling her face as he touched
her lips
Caresses she longed for from him who over thousands of days had told
the stars

Of his love for her through his long suffering weighed on him fifty years
through
Authored blame lashed out at him since a boy now a man with redeemed
sorrows

Calling her home to his weathered hands holding her gently kissing her softly
Why didn't she marry him he wants to know a boy of seventeen so
long ago?

 18

THE ANNIVERSARY

Overcast clouds in grays skim the horizon kissing the meeting of the
ocean walking

On rain dotted web printed sand as slow crashing waves with soft foam
melt into

The inlets left by night time visitors her feet knowing the direction to
where they met.

Sitting on the wall left by the worshipers of the sun now at their routine
of living for

Today she lifts the perfect feathers strewn about the perimeter
unconcerned to the

Reason for their laying amid the coughed up treasures she seeks for his
grave's

Adornment speaking to him of her undying love crying with droplets of
rain on her face

Seeking a most perfect stone heart shaped to hold in her hand close to
her breast

In a few brief meetings their love was formed for eternity, how could she
know

She was his forever as he whispered to her soul his undying words loving
her only

To ravish her soul through the spirals of time hearing his voice in the
quiet of noise

Of crashing sea droplets merging the crevices made ravine-like in inlets
of oceans

THE THROW AWAY

Stashed in bins in corners of the darkened lab the petrified remains of
fetuses cast out of

Un-readied wombs lay motionless in brine. Maybe trillions aborted since
the decision to

Take away life un-started. That debate rises and falls like the heaps of
recycled trash in

Myriads of plants cross country protecting the environment for future
generations of

Forsaken souls whose lives were foreshortened by avarice and greed
pontificated.

When is the decision made to mark the throw away? Who is weighted
so heavily with

Power of pen in authorization to decide who cannot stay in living to die
in ignominy?

Has the decision been made before their own beginning? If so who is so
powered?

Where then goes the soul? Not completed for living does it wander the
bowels of hell?

Or searches the fathoms of oceans, faceless and deformed; seeking the
face of God?

Insight finds the throw away marked at any age, also aborted are; the
two year old, the

ten year old, the thirty or eighty year old all decided for elimination from
ordinary life.

At any age someone in power can eliminate the timid, the disenfranchised
by treachery

How would they know? Since they do not plunder but trust, do not reap
but give.

Labeled weak and useless easily fooled fervently trusting should they be
eliminated?

Righteousness grounds noble sentiments churning the thinking of the
   tyrant making
Rounds on the deathbeds labeled for extinction claiming to die before
   their time
Noble piety resounds it is their karma and they will get their just due not
   to worry least
They rebel raising the doors of hell in anticipation of freedom not given
   for promises
Made being fooled for eternity denied lives they righteously earned from
   brokers of time.

AFRAID TO DIE

Proud and indignant claiming all the righteousness and power from the
very beginning
Why shouldn't he think he is owed the intimacies he craves and believes
it is his due
Developing his plan with intricacies thought through with shrewd and
clever cunning.

She would never know too naïve and trusting easily fooled into thinking
he is sincere
Needing to believe he would love her forever a fool to most and gullible
if deceived
Years upon years in deception coaching his ego while goading her insecurity.

No one would blame him he tells himself relentless in his endless passions
Feeding his insatiable urges don't change the catheter Betty warns 'he'll
be dead
By Tuesday', 'do you really want to hurt him', as she scanned for any
valuables,

Her eyes darting across the dining room 'why would you want to do
that', 'you'll have
To pay for the ambulance' while passing the bag across the laced table
in a gesture
Speaking of defeat losing the battle to claim the devil's soul with ransomed
suffering

JUST LAYING IN THE ROAD

Just laying in the road, still
He was well dressed
Shoes with no scuffs
Maybe he knew where he'd be
At the end of the day
What was he thinking?
With guns drawn and
Willing to shoot it out
Willing to die
Why are some heroes outlaws?
He had the courage to go
It alone to the end
Was he dead inside already?
Was it his destiny?

IN A HALLWAY

Jagged pieces lay splintered in a broken frame.
I mourn your needless death;
Your final gift fell on un-requited arms
To revenge for justice due is no more a cause.

Pointed jagged edges that no longer know a home:
Sit gathered in the dust bin, were it not for all
The tall cathedral spires;
Would broken colored pieces find a resting place?

So some small shaft of light might reach this core,
Pour molten lead on shattered broken pieces,
To make a window only for the light;
Not a reflection cast by gleaming precious stone,

Nor sun danced raindrops on a mountainside,
Make some small transparency so light might pass.
Labor not to refit the pieces, their task is finished in their former state.
A very tiny corner of a chapel proves to be a greedy selfish dream; instead

Insert within a portal, in a hallway darkened by the greed of man,
Where the masses pass in knowing and unknowing
To filter light for other broken frames;
To be there like the morning!

LIFE'S ATONEMENT

How can I stop the raging?
The door only opens inward.
Once inside this unnamed anger
Tears at the moorings of my very soul
Wrecking havoc, breeding distress,
Disquiet and chaos

I choose to form the words
But no one claims them,
Heaping them back upon me in insult and indemnity
Who are the just of this world?
Why is so large a measure of all good things theirs?
Their backs have not broken from burdens assumed of their goodness.

They have not paid in pleading and in gnawing
Their eyes burst with tears of dryness
They cry in silence so they say
But I have never seen their tears of joy
Shed for sheer delight
Only glory seems to be their lot.

THE BETRAYER'S DECEPTION

It is you that I deny
For you have betrayed me
You once held open the doors to solitude and comfort
Believing all your nuances, intuitions;
Loving when all reason vanished,
Trusting that good would conquer over hate
You have betrayed me.....
You who gave me life and freedom
Now freedom is usurped by fear
And constant tears swell behind my eyes.
O trusted friend, O self I need you,
Meet me where I have put up the wall.
I long for yesterday in all its' goodness,
Knowing that my joyous innocence is past
Unite this frame of bone and blood unto you.
One cannot trust two masters
Believing one above the other,
It is now I who deny you...
I am now the betrayer!

CROSSING INTO DYING

How fooled we were to think it would make us be eternal
To live among the sainted ones who do no harm while
Crossing into dying quoting scripted passages
Their glories dredge the earth of song and goodness.

What waits them least they think their abstinence
Sainted them for heaven's chores of living amongst
The wicked not faring the tolls of the sorrowed
They too are lying in the road while crossing into dying

NIGHTWATCH

Humbled bent and pleading,
Imploring for the faintest glimmer,
Wretched broken man
One word one blinking of an eye redeems him.
More than one or tens of millions of
Light years of time and space
Held tight by not so much as
A silken thread

Uncompromising thought, and added fear
Bind him in this narrow fringe of being.
Surround; encompass him, of all you are.
Forgiveness brings a speedy death,
To despairing ponderings
You who share night's sleep and
Knit the firmament of ocean bottom
Cast out my soul's own murderer.

WALKING IN THE CITIES
OF THE DEAD

At each corner turns the pavement when the thunder quickens skies in
tears
For who knows the dead who walk the paths in hallways for marked souls
Stirring recollections for the chosen what waste in thinking they are
saved.
Spare no costs in undoing the preconceptions least they flaunt their
holiness

And lose sight of do gooding for the sake of the suffering at times ending.
Taking back their urges in occupations wanderings nets the coveted
prizes
So much of wasted lives seeking glories for their greed and selfishness
Bearing witness to their wasted wealth lavishing themselves in riches

Leaving impoverished looted lands and swollen ravaged bellies emptied
To suffer the indiscretions of the of their greed what care they who they
Trample or mane for their self serving in the name of righteousness to wet
Their avarice for justice is their own undoing with malice in fated
godlessness

MY SOUL KNOWS YOUR NAME

In the darkest regions and in arid deserts
Anticipation of a glimmer of your face
Harkens legions upon legions quaking
Majesties and constellations of thrones

And Seraphim in galvanized wailing
In times past my soul knelt in reverence while
Nard the fragrant balsam permeated the rafters
Of totem markings on blackened offerings

Spliced in time immortal waiting for the son
Heralds trumpeting messages of joyous news
He comes to shouts he is risen he is risen
Hallelujah alleluia in the name of all that is holy

A WHISPER OF WIND

Shelves of books line the library of the school trying to pick one not too
    thick in order to
Finish the report the nun asked on lives of the saints squinting at the neat
    rows there is
Maria Goretti a young girl in Italy who was raped not even knowing the
    meaning why
It was small and would be over and done to get it finished at 9 not much
    of a Catholic

At least she recalls how most of the nuns hated the ancestry why she
    wondered all the
Ignominy not enough aware at 14 to understand that she was discriminated
    against a
Pattern that would be her entire life even though so beautiful more than
    she suspected
following her into a marriage based on lust for another whose sins she
    would forgive

Recalling other sainted ones thinking a martyr is what she asked for
    herself from God
He would never answer her prayers so she didn't have to worry but he is
    the same one
Who brought her into the light knowing her deepest soul saving all the
    candy to share at
Five before he bathe her in his light taking her most prized possessions
    swaddled

In balm and buried in dirt never to lend their heart to comfort her tears
    reaching across
Time forever leaving her alone in the plasters walking the stations

THANKS FOR THE MAIL

Peeking out from the cellophane of the pictured pages it reads: *A.C. King*
Your satisfaction is my pleasure: knowing ahead of time that he made an
Impression built on a reputation aimed to insure work was done to his
   specifications
Catching her eye as he hoped her seeing him hanging from the upper
   bunk in blues

A gorgeous man...... a Hunk...... known for his charm and persuasion
   loved for
His sensuous kisses his charming ways and his incredible dancing, how
   could you
Not melt in his embrace yearning to thank her for all of the presents sent
   him at a time
When he needed them most to confirm he was loved far the best of
   them all

KILL ME QUICK

Kill me quick least I suffer the rancid pain of your done deeds
Spare me the flash of your heinous sword darken the path of its swathe
Cover my wounds with roses spent, leak not the marrow of my bones
Nor drench the blood from my veins, for I see thee in memories past

Washing the wounds so easily severed burning the flesh torn from the bone
Staining the wood with sinew shattered with fashioned lathe and shackled
    flesh
Twisting the emptied shell of man of holy memory and kindness deeds bound
Layering the spoils on narrow planks to sea least contempt be bargained
    to god

FIVE YEARS

It's like she just died but she has been gone forever....I never grew up I'm still like a kid Only a few good memories live in my head she used to drink Tab do they still make Tab? She made me like broccoli, she used to let me drink her coffee, she would get mad when I would drink it. I wanted to soak up every minute of her, it was like I knew ahead of time I wasn't going to have her for long. She would take us to Mac Donald's as a treat but she never ate I don't know why; "asking her mommy why aren't you eating"?

He was always cheating on her, she would cry, then buy new clothes for us and never anything for herself...she never did. I must have ripped out 36 pages...gone..... I glued the cover back on. All the places where I should have been I'm not. Twenty two years; a lifetime for many. I couldn't promise her, I know I should have, I caused her to kill herself, if I only had said yes, she would be alive. Over and over I go over the small memories locked in my brain, how old would she be now? that I'm 37 almost the age

she killed herself when I didn't go to save her when I didn't say I'm sorry mom, but you know what he is doing, you know how afraid I am, I can't go through that anymore. I can't let him rape me anymore. I need to have a life. I need to stop being afraid all the time. Did you know I burn my arms, it started when you died, no suicided, how could you have killed yourself. ....why wasn't I enough to keep you alive? Am I that hopeless? That you too want to leave me? I want to leave me all the time, covered in leaves on a

rocky hillside...by the low side of the cliff where sky predators rip at my flesh and shred me to bone....on the edge of the ocean to drift out to sea....or wander the continents with never a home deserving of none for the sins I have done...or cast out to perish for times immortal

dredging earth's longings in exchange for my soul to keep you from dying is that not enough to keep you my mother.....to remember my longing at the side of your Grave... to lay down beside you in the crook of your arm and the wound where you died.

A TOUGH DECISION

Between the layers of opinion covered in gilded patterns
Whether right nor left side wins; the decision becomes a
Pattern of life long practice; and sometimes endured patience
Getting to choose first is what counts

The shape remains imprinted on muslin like weavings
For a decision lingering on the morning of the event
Is pronounced the winner gaining momentum in privileged circles
To be swaddled tucked and folded

TO BE RIGHT

No other destination nor plan can be as perfect as being right
What is all the fuss about what do you care if you know the truth
What difference does it make that there are many sides
You need to win no matter what
What do you mean there is another view
The best position is the right side

VOICES

Only a voice gives the deepest tones of sorrow and sadness
Embellishing the breathing with husky soul
Moore tells the story of forgiving as soul deep,
Is this the voice he speaks?
Letting the bellows bounce off windpipes and chandeliers
Of god feared men in gowned attire
Standing at the cross with flames burning treetops
Hanged in error shouts
Fall amidst the broken smudge
Of burning flesh forgiven

DESERT WALKER

Stands tall among men as their comrade
A tree trunk of a man towering muscled
Poised for action
The gentlest of a soul with invading knowing eyes

Labored in sun drenched tones by the evening sun
Could not have known his destiny nor played a role
In his demise
Instead he fortuned his own strength to win the ending

Growing from boy to man on seas at seventeen
Scarred by the sacredness of mother's love and belted beatings
Sheltered by his youth
Questioned why he was not loved by either

How much more could he have given, how harder could he have tried
Always longing for the unconditional
How he yearned
To be the favored son, accepted without guilt

What great gift of unconditional love weaved in longing
Intent on every word every nuance
Filling the spaces
Of the soul's own darkness glistening in their meeting

Giving the greatest of his marrow
Memories etched in crystals
Sparkling hearings
Matched beatings of hearts in souls united

Befriended in the barren desert wasteland walker
No relief against the enemies
Braved with unsuspecting
Courage to stand against the doors of hell

No finding our way back to the land of living
Now sustained on blinking lights in water bubbles dancing
In the corners
Hanging in the shadows

COMMON GRAVE

The iris and azalea lay buried in their common grave
No more to sing the beauty of the sun
Or stand in countenance to receive the rain
I mourn your needless death.

They died before their time heaped under
Mounds of shoveled earth. Eighteen years
Of careful tending watching every tiny glow
Of color exclaiming wonder at their yearly birth

You grew and multiplied beyond belief
She said you wouldn't grow so could I use you
Heavy with child and unskilled in the art of planting
I rushed to plant you so you would not die in vain

Part of me has died with you for not only for
Your beauty do I mourn but your presence
Spoke to me of all creation in quiet
Communion you testified all beings

In times of wholeness past
You weaned me from the paths of idleness
And schooled me in the paths of gentleness
To grieve your death is all that's left to me

POETRY

Words have no meaning
The spaces in between tell all the story

BEYOND THE FACE

No amount of telling
Penetrates the ears of those who will not hear
No amount of begging to be understood brings about acceptance.
Not so much a flicker of what used to be remains,
The glass conspires in recriminations' pact.
Find a label, lay the blame, so what's an inability to cope;
Just another way to herd the masses!
Externals convey the levies of the torments or the ecstasy
Not all who live choose for power, or wield in force.
Not all want to control the world.......but instead to cherish it,
To hold it close......to recreate on each new morning
The wonder of the person!

THIS OUR PRECIOUS SON

Cool water runs over tiny toes splashing in the warm sand how amazing
to look at this

glorious child so perfect in every way so splendid without imperfections
without flaws

Our hearts catch each other's glance thinking how fortunate we are to
have created this

Beautiful child weaving in and out of the circle of the sun draped in
sparkling shadows

Glowing in the path of justice in the cities of reason and academies of law
and science

Giving us his parents glory where we reach heights of adulation not
meant of our doing

May you never feel the pain of sorrow we pray our precious son so loyal
so handsome

Growing in wisdom your gift growing in holiness we never captured
until now we vision

You in the path of grace with forefathers leading you home armed with
valor forsaking

sorrows and broken heartedness basking in the light eternal in the
majesties of ancients

Drawing you in to the holy of holies keeping the promise granting you
graces fulfilling

The prayers in God ever lasting may you never feel the cold of winter
loving you always

MAY YOU NEVER FEEL
THE COLD OF WINTER

May you never feel the winter cold on feet once warmed in mother's hands
Of rocking chairs and cradle swings as your soul unfolds in angle's wings

May you never feel the scorching heat of desert winds and moving sands
Of blowing grains in crystal mesh on folding wraps of golden beams

As ancients wait to welcome you with arms festooned with blossoms swell
They tell the tale of new made souls in galleried fashioned gleaming light

Of leafy glen and mountain side in ocean rush of waves marooned in passer by
Now bear me well they want to know how many dreams they do foretell

May you never know the purple rain that falls amidst the blackened ash of
Suffered souls forsaken sins anointing grants their saving grace

May you never know the pain of sin forsaken God whose mercies grow in
Saving you for ransomed souls

HOT ICE

Excitement bounced out of the radio words telling the happy stories of
    independence

Shared spaces with bands and singing and all that made up the revelry
    of flags and

Beaches filled with noise and sand and lazy summer holidays these are
    the times

That make us remember the ones who gave us this freedom the ones
    who gave

Us the blessings all gathered in slogans the "war is over" "the war is over"
    rang on

Towers and tree tops and balconies lined up the push carts on cobbled
    streets molted

With bantered sales of fireworks exploding in patches of lawn away from
    the fields

Spilling the sounds raising the flags on the fourth of July holding the
    Hoodsies in hot ice

THE JOURNEY

From young to old was not a pleasant journey, not for me
It all went too fast and I am left with empty bones
Hollow at the middle, scraped clean. There seems to be no
Future in my future, in my past there's a hazy memory;

Most of it lost, most of the people lost. People I thought I
Would be with forever, now gone or just disappeared.
And I am alone. I do not mind being alone, most of the time.
But some of the time I have a longing to connect with someone

Or something, but I can't figure it out. The world seems to be running
Too fast for me, part of a sprint I could never compete with.
And once again I am left behind with self doubt and self hate
I go day by day waiting for my death, not knowing how I feel.

DYING ALONE

Somehow we never expected it to be this way
But as we gain on this side of life
We grow increasingly narrow in whom we can trust
So the numbers dwindle coming to the end

Of those we befriended by the side of the bridge
Deciding if we will let them in to the meager shell
That only exists to pick apart the sacred giftings
Cast aside by limited grace and empty hallows

In back alleys the strays wait for the final crumbs
Knowing their time is limited not counting graces
Or done deeds makes them less dependent on the
Mercies of God instead weighing their sufferings

God appears more accepting of their limitations
In exchange for their redemption He anoints them
Blessing them with waters and oils of the Spirit
Marking them His with forgiveness sanctifying

Them of sins created of broken mind and spirit now
Pouring forth the holiness they seek in mind and soul
And body in Blood and Water gushing forth into the
Font bringing them into the fold of God Almighty

BENEDICTUS

In the name of all that is holy calling forth legions, mea culpa, mea culpa
Bowing in the name of the Lord hiding in the bowels of hell shredding
The pages sewn with grace to ease the seeking of graces believed in the
Coming in the name of the Lord to sanctify the masses of believers

Giving God his due in penances.

THE ANOINTING

Told to come to the front railing on the left, he would give her the bottle
of Holy Water

Genuflecting on one knee as low to the ground is no longer with ease
her bones tell her

Kneeling is without ease where once she did so in easy penance but now;
stiffened with

Time, and aging she knows God knows there is no more ease to doing
what is needed.

Controlled anger evident, she questions the urgency and the demand to
kneel in position

The game plan has changed, he perjures himself claiming her possession
with evil, he

Insists he will do justice, certain of the mark which labels her soul forsaken
not ransomed

He buys her forgiveness needed to be sainted and anointed as a priest to
ransom souls.

SNOW

Crystalizing
Mesmerizing
Tantalizing
Energizing
Vitalizing
Synthesizing
Synchronizing
Memorizing
Tranquilizing
Invigorating
Scintillating
Felicitating
Reparation
Affiliation
Expatriation
Association
Asphyxiation
Respiration
Falling
Calling
Flowing
Flow
Ice
Ice Flow
Frozen
Sleep
Dying...........

IN COBALT BLUE

Slipping in on the left side of the cobalt blue
Pressed and buttoned layered in position for
Now seven months both arms folded round
Held in tightly least he not forget he is loved

For all time immortal conceived at their union
Wedged between longings and conceptions
Times would take her breath away the fancies
Of loving a soldier for becoming a hero to country

Her intentions faithful for promises whispered
On the left shoulder surrounded by satin white
In layers perfumed in passed flowers known
For their true love circled in white carnations

True to never let him sleep alone she draws him
Close tears filling the seamed markings of the
Bright radiance of medaled ribbons testifying his
Solidarity in corps to his dying words on bloodied

Paper writing her name in undying love for all
To see her pressing him closely to his child she
Is carrying under the canopy of layered white satin
Tear stained remembrances shrouded in cobalt blue.

THE SEARCH

Long ago in Nonni's bed
Visions of I used to be
Swim in my head.
A young girl mirrors in my eye
She cannot stop the searching
Not knowing what she seeks.
Weave the ribbons of a former time
Looking yet never finding
She knows she holds the answer,
She knows she is the last
A long time quiet intervenes

WHO DO I REDEEM?

Could this meager minute of a life have only been in vain?
Countless shatterings and batterings, no restitution
Who is it that I redeem?
I ask not proof but understanding
A glimpse to keep me going on,
The journey's past through needles eye;
But knows no ending
Have I come that I should only seek and seek?
Never finding only seeking!
Annihilation for a just reward!

LIKE THE ALABASTER RAIN

Life spent in mirrored images
Long past and overdue,
Snatched between promise and expectation
For courage never comes to those who wait on shadows
Illusion or delusion, whichever hushes real
Dust capped remnants of a life
Reminders of a former wholeness past
Pressing to hold on, and refusing to let go!

PANIC OF THE MIND

In the journey into night
All terrors that were ever dreamed appear
Life sized horrors chocked the daily mainstream
Wracking soul, and mind and body
Disintegration!
In mind's eye all visions faded into panic
The executioner has severed every bone;
From muscle blood and tendon
Now observer and prisoner both I be!

THE OTHER ME

In the place where once your shadow stood,
Insanity now masquerades as person!

INTEGRATION

Hell has found a balance
The self is beginning to love
The storm and the raging has ended
Quiet floods the merging.
A whisper of the wind
Is all that stands between

IN MID SEASON

With all my might and power
I struggle to keep out the rain
Pounding soaking, piercing rain
No washing and no balming

Terror dread and fearful rain!
This tree of man has now become
Alike the torrid steaming jungle forest!
I give up to you my shade, and

You also take my dew and branches,
Hulking at me as though I feel no pain
Nothing that I offer
Ever satisfies your thirst.

You rest against my trunk, and plot to
Splinter me to wood,
Lifeless trunk from which all sap has drained.
Torrid rain to rip out broken roots;

No shade, no rest, no arm against the storm.
O life beyond my life, send your gentle calming rain!
Wash from me which was and is into the stream of living!
Make new a remnant for that which is to come

THE INVITATION

Come into this my dwelling place
For this is truly where I live.
Be not afraid of its darkness
For cool running springs
Line its passageways.
Let your shattered mind rest in its' unknowing;
Draw from the well of my gentleness,
Cover your spent weariness with my mantle,
Release to me your long shouldered burden,
Rest and await the sunrise!

THE SURVIVOR

In quiet sandy beaches
And barren desert wastelands
Crimson leafed wanderers trod silently,
Stripped of paths and homeland
Ghetto camped survivor without a place to rest.

CONCENTRATION

COULD BE THE MEDS.........
COULD BE THE PAIN.........
TWISTED THOUGHTS THAT LEAVE US HELPLESS
ALL TRYING IN OUR WAY TO UNDERSTAND

BUBBLES! EXPLODING! POPPING IN MY MIND
BUT I CAN LEARN
I CAN BE HUMAN AND RELATE
SO MANY I D'S WHO DO THEY SAY I AM?

DIZZINESS, TWISTING, PRESSED AGAINST OUR WILL
CONCENTRATION, MIXED VOICES
DISTRUSTING THOUGHTS WRACK MY BEING
HOW WILL I EVER GET APPROVED
IF I SPACE OUT AT THE WHEEL?

WAITING FOR THE KILL

Rippled watered edges lap
Sentiments and sting memories
Fastened still with uncut cords
Beneath the surface
The enigma waits empty handed
In awe and trembling of the god-mountain
Anger's author assigns the unending blame
A task at which he bears
The stamp of righteousness;
Poised in ever readiness.
To strike the killing blow!

THE THROWAWAY BRIDE

Plotted from the beginning fitting a plan for a Mafioso dictator
Never deviating from the decision to be the first for a throwaway bride
Whims and whimsical thinking guides the denial of the Mafiosa.

JUSTIFICATION

This time I won't let it happen
The door to my self once a refuge
Has now become the door to my
Very own hell laying bare the years
Of hurt and blame to the core of my
Being leaving nothing more for
Fighting or for healing, turning upon
Itself and splintering every bone
Not until the last drop of blood is shed
Does it merge in token victory
This time I won't let it happen
This time I'll break down the door

INSIDE

Oh God some think that only the best part of their self is what is due you
But you know the self that rages for you created it as the side of the whole
In this clay of person remold the two as one for at the core is goodness

PAID

The fault has to be found with me so your world can stay in focus
Why does it fall on me to do the bleeding? Why must you make
me the casualty for your living? Your so called power and strength
are not your own but have been paid for with my life

CORNERED PREY

Fear enslaves me to the rhythm of the moment;
Grasping, wretched, paralyzing
No door to open for relief.
Stalking, pinned unto a wall
Terror seizes all my consciousness,
Reason fades replaced by panic;
Locked in a prison
Without walls or key
Willing that your will be done,
The un-surmounting mountain
Barricades me
Sharp, piercing cliffs and precipices
Form stanchions for the un-walled cell.
I can't go on
No resources left to scale the gorge;
Resisting, refusing to push on,
Wounded, bleeding, lying in a pool of blame
Tortured to the core of being,
Death is the only refuge left to me.

REFLECTIONS IN A SPIRAL

Are you only as much as we think we are?
Ponderings stretch the now and after
Seeking you alone who satisfies our yearning
The three parts never reconciled unto the other.
Intuition says your presence holds the answer
The morning sun knows your face
And winter's darkest chill feels your warmth.

BROKEN GENESIS

Worn cragged bony ridges,
wrinkled furrowed windows to the sea,
pained beyond your time
No stone or blood writing
deems your suffocating death.
Alone to squalor in your loss
never having had a life,
dependent for your daily bread.
Some reap and plunder never turn a face
not redemption, just sad ignomy.
Nameless mirrors to the portal deep
lifeless, taut, and deep-set eyes,
thrashing ocean upon ocean
Stir the waters spirit hand.

BEYOND THE FACE

No amount of telling
penetrates the ears of those who will not hear.
No amount of begging to be understood brings about
acceptance.
Not so much a flicker of what used to be
remains,
the glass conspires in recrimination's pact.
Find a label, lay the blame
so what's an inability to cope
just another way to herd the mass.
Externals convey the levies of the torments
or the esctacies.
Not all who live choose for power
or wield in force.
Not all want to control the world.....
but instead to cherish it,
to hold it close,
to recreate on each new morning,
the wonder of the person.

Words have no meaning
the spaces in between
tell all the story.

Tongueless voices echo in the canyons
seasoned years
mellowed words fleeting
barren wombless scars screaming
borrowed spirit growns
thinking it had past

As I'm dying and I'm crying
for the new life kept
from trying
groans the borrowed spirit
sighing---
who would know?

THE FIRST SNOW

Glistening in soft whispers
Changing contours or rounds and squares
New blanket to cover the dirtied land
For tiny minutes what was worn and broken
Receives anew a christening robe
Swelling and gale tossed to frigid force
Wet and chapped, meeting ice and skin

THE FIRST SNOW

Glistening in soft whispers
changing contours of rounds and squares,
new blanket to cover the dirtied land.
For tiny minutes what was worn and broken
receives anew a christening robe.
Swelling and gailing to frigid force
wet and chapped, meeting ice and skin
breathes deep, the falling healing fountain.
Arising life of origin's mistake
inhales the god-spirit from pore to pore
    "anointed fallen man
    take comfort in my grace
    this small watered symbol
    knows no boundaries of my love
    I imaged you to me
    you who are my very tears
    I cannot wash you from me
    in daystars time: I will remember you."

INTEGRATION

Hell has found a balance
The self is beginning to love,
the storm and the raging is ended,
Quiet floods the merging.

NIGHTWATCH

Having paid the ransom
more than 70 times 7.
It's debt continues to be metered out
in further executions.
The best of silver and of gold
will never be its equal,
nor that of poultry bones
and bleeding flesh.
Wrapped in a flag of white,
the dreams and hopes which maybe
could have been;
speak of no surrender for the tyrant.
What's left of broken mind and spirit
fallen wax lays heaped and moulded
round a tiny flame,
smoke long carried to the four creation
A whisper of the wind
is all that stands between.

REFLECTIONS IN A SPIRAL

Are you only as much as we think
we are?
Ponderings stretch the now and after
Seeking you alone who satisfies our yearning
the 3-parts never reconciled unto the other.
Intuition says your presence holds the answer;
the morning sun knows your face
and winter's darkest chill,
feels your warmth.
humbled, bent and pleading,
imploring for the faintest glimmer,
wretched, broken man
One word, one blinking of an eye redeems him.
more than one, or tens of millions'
light years of time and space;
held tight by not so much
a silken thread.
Uncompromising thought, and added fear
bind him in this narrow fringe of being.
Surround, encompass him, of all you are
forgiveness brings a speedy death
to despairing ponderings.
You who share night's sleep and
knit the firmament of ocean bottom
cast out my soul's own murderer

FORSAKEN

I BELIEVE HE HAS FORSAKEN ME
THE REASONS WHY I CANNOT SEE
HE'S HELD MY HAND IN TIMES OF WOE
BUT NOW HE'S CHOSE TO LET IT GO
TO TURN HIS BACK ON ALL MY PRAYERS
SOMETIMES I WONDER IF HE'S THERE
BUT THERE'S THE STILL SMALL VOICE
WITHIN ME DECLARES
BELIEVE IN HIM, BELIEVE IN HIM
BELIEVE IN HIM THAT WAS CRUCIFIED
THE NAILS IN HIS HANDS, THE TEARS IN HIS EYES
WHO DID ALL THIS TO SET YOU FREE?
THAT FATE-FILLED DAY AT CALVARY.

BUT THEN I THINK, IS THIS AN ILLUSION
THAT STILL SMALL VOICE
DOES IT KNOW OF SECLUSION?
OF BEING TIED DOWN IN A BED OVERNIGHT
WITH NOTHING OVERHEAD BUT A LIGHT.
FIGHTING THOUGHT OF SELF-DESTRUCTION
PRAYING TO A GOD, HOPING, TRUSTING.
SHOCK TREATMENTS THAT YOU TRIED TO FIGHT
THOUGHTS OF THEM AS YOU WATCH THE LIGHT

IN A LITTLE ROOM SO DARK AND BARE
WITHOUT EVEN A SIGN OF A CHAIR
OF OVERDOESE AND SCARS SELF-INFLICTED
OF DRUGS THAT TO SOME HAVE BECOME ADDICTIVE
OF STATE INSTITUTIONS, WHERE SOME ARE DESTINED TO LIVE
BECAUSE OF WHAT?
WHAT EXCUSE CAN IT GIVE?

THE HEALING WOMAN

You speak of love and show in signs and symbols
The shapes and forms that you will use to show your love
Where is the love for this person who lays bleeding within
If it were not for her your life would have ended years before

Give her the best that you once gave to others, reach out to hold her
She heals the wounds of many, and cries their hushed tears
She is the fiber and marrow of your bones.

THE ONLY DEFECTIVE

She lives in morning sunsets
seagulled oceanfronts
amassed emotions tuggings
crumpled memories luggings
footprinted Jamaican beaches
wistful wonderings
cocoon nuturings pebbled
captured in an inkling

Rippled watered edges lap
sentiments and stinging memories
fastened still with uncut cords
Beneath the surface the inigma
waits empty handed
in awe and trembling of the god-mountain
Angers author assigns the unending blame
a task at which he bears
the stamp of righteousness,
poised in ever-readiness
to strike the killing blow.

THE OTHER DEFECTIVE

She lives in morning sunsets
seagulled ocean fronts
amassed emotions tuggings
crumpled memories luggings
footprinted Jamaican beaches
wistful wonderings
cocoon nurturings pebbled
captured in an inkling.

May the floor of this house
bring strength to the feet

May the ceiling provide
shelter from life's troubles

May the wind of encouragement
blow across these windowpanes

May the hallways
dance with laughter

May the air be filled with gladness

Forevermore

Printed in the United States
By Bookmasters